WELCOME TO THE BRIGHT SIDE

Didactic Poetry

ATIQA Z. RIZVI

Title: Welcome To The Bright Side
Language: English
Character set encoding: UTF-8

First published by

An Imprint of BlueRose Publishers

Head Office: B-6, 2nd Floor,
ABL Workspaces, Block B, Sector 4,
Noida, Uttar Pradesh 201301
M: +91-8882 898 898

Dedication

**I dedicate my write-up to my family for being
constantly supportive and making me feel better
each passing day.**

Acknowledgements

I thank Allah (God) for letting me fulfill my childhood dream of becoming a published author/writer followed by thanking my publisher Blue Rose and its CEO Mr. Syed Arshad.

The people I need to thank are a lot and for various kind and pure reasons. Some of their names are as follows :

Mr. Ashir Rizvi (Big brother)

Mr. Qaisar Abbas (uncle)

Mr. Faisal Sayed (brother)

Mr. Ronald Lewis (Professor)

Ms. Suniti Pethe (My favourite Professor)

Mr. Sudhakar Solomonraj (Professor)

Ms. Anjali Masarguppi (Professor)

Ms. Lorraine Ramos (Professor)

Mr. Mahesh Shetti (Professor)

Ms. Vinita Mathew (Professor)

Mr. Shominlun Lhungdim (friend)

Ms. Sharon Robert (friend)

Mr. Glen Aloysius (friend)

Mr. Seigunlien Khongsai (friend)

Mr. Chandan Prajapati (friend)

Ms. Takam Oku (friend)

Ms. Bommik Koyu Bogum (friend)

Ms. Zingxhonphy Zimik (friend)

Mr. Shiva Chinnaswamy (friend)

Ms. Kajol Tamang (friend)

Ms. Sonali Panickar (best friend)

Ms. Satya Prakasham (friend)

Mr. Chawngsangzuala Zote (friend)

x

Foreword

It's a book that deserves to be on every shelf . . .

- Mrs. Suniti A. Pethe.

XII

Preface

Welcome To The Bright Side is a continuation to The Flip Side Of Poetry by Atiqa Z. Rizvi. It is a collection of 24 didactic poems which teach and instruct about life. It can be read by any age group.

XIV

Prologue

Understanding life through poems.

XVI

Contents

How's Life ?

Life is good, God is great. I just hope, my prayers don't get answered too late. Lately I've learned to appreciate. I could still scribble on my slate like I do with my pen on pages these days. I feel super safe in my den.

Is it important to lose something so precious, that it can't be replaced to have life figured out? Just being me but the world keeps being mean. Not just to me, but everybody I see around me. It gets contagious, you see?

I am keen to know the differences too, but respectfully.

Think I have a fragile mind, full of stupidity, I have been pitied for keeping the heart clean. All I know is

He's been merciful to you and me.

It's a gift from Him so I'd rather try not to complain about it.

Even if situation and times get hard, and there seems no signs of positivity. Little love, affection and support can lead to blooming flowers on a barren tree.

It's dry, looks dead from far away. Not a single new leaf is detected, but if you look closely there are flowers blossoming. Almost like summing up life for me and you.

- AZR

Perfect Facade

Rulers make the rules to their own benefits. Choosers will choose for their own credits.

Our ideas don't match and fit, but we love the location to bits. It's a cheaper vacation spot and the animations make us laugh often and a lot. We just want to get less spotted and there is no place spotless.

Nation being sold, vaccinations being bought, the slots were booked. Unrest arised. Others became bold and nothing had them shook. Amidst adversity some played roles of the crooked.

Common people are doomed it's still assumed.

The maturity of organizing girls and the power of charming boys is the need of the hour for all.

Some have been fighting the fraught and battling in a long term war.

We forfeit at times as the seeds have been sown centuries ago. Sun shone brightly every single time though. Men tell it's mental, Women tell it's heartfelt.

Neighbours said they've got no chill, the calamities they dealt with wasn't easy. They've got to pay a list of unending bills. The paper has been crumpled and dropped in the bin, how it is wished that could clean few of the sins.

Does that ring a bell in the head or are we still concentrating on the jewelled rings lying on the bed? While we sing and don't hung onto every word it's true but dead stones, infact, artifacts, decorated like some of our ideologies and ideals. Something needs to be dug deeper than the mines. Our minds and hearts needs a crystal clear and pristine polish shine time to time.

- AZR

23

Clickbait

When we think we click and decide to stick together and take it forward but in the middle find things way too different from what was initially perceived.

That we somehow got tricked by our own feelings and the novelty of people and places in our tender ages. The edges or the surface completely tend to be opposite as compared to the depth and core at times.

The awesome folks or venues we go to all appear with messier views when you have a closer look. It would be better if we accept the harsh truth and empathize and say, we are not perfect either.

There is a need to not worry what others think, to not feel guilty and believe things get better with time, space and experiences. We just have to know if it's worthy of our precious investments.

The truth Is nobody is already too smart and hardworking from birth, we all grow and built together over time with the help of other people around. We grasp energies. Independency is great but dependency is a normal trait.

So, if it feels like a clickbait, don't get annoyed or disappointed. It all comes together and flourishes in the end.

- AZR

My Only Prayer

I only pray and yearn for pleasant days. No extreme heights. Stable phase, calm and peaceful sights. The taste of stillness and togetherness. Falling of dry flowers and leaves. Growing back of the new ones in the same place. Less hibernation, instead.

Occasional cool breeze on hot summer days. Either familiar face or location if I tend to go somewhere on a distant vacation, just in case. The feeling of contentment is eventually entering mine and my beloved's mind, I guess.

- AZR

Let You Know

Is it worth it to let you know I saw you in a dream of mine last night? Everything felt so right with you just besides. You were the reason when I opened my eyes as I came back to life, I smiled.

They say a sleeping person's scenario is a lot like the dead. Except for the fact, there is a heart beating in their chest and a subconscious mind which is cruel and sometimes kind. As we rest, a sweet dream or nightmare, is anybody's guest.

Would it be okay if I let you know I wish to see you once again tonight even if it's just in a dream of mine? Although for a longer time, this time. Reality isn't as pretty as it seems while we are a bit younger to still believe that the grass is always green on the other side.

Does it sound right if I let you know it transcends me back to the past? As I sit and retrospect and be deeply nostalgic, like a lot.

Am I overthinking or simply thinking, would someone diagnose this feeling as a problem just because the topic to talk is so current, contagious and hot?

If I let you know, the reason behind those tears is nothing specific but a collection of mixed memories of love and hurt. I hate to admit I'm unassertive when I speak but can be real direct and clear when I scrib onto a paper or a screen while my fingers do all the dancing.

If only I let you know, would you be kinder towards others than before? Would you deal patiently and know that no one is perfect and pros and cons is a universal trait.

- AZR

28

Rise And Shine

As the days get cold and the memories get old, I hope you keep yourself warm under your favourite coat.

At the breaking dawn, avoid breaking down.

Instead, rise and shine like the Sun over your head each morning and when it's gone for its time would come, move ahead with grace like the pretty replacement of the sparkling sky that follows through the night. Often wondering why? Trust your best is yet to come, you're worth all that wait. It's never too late.

Meanwhile, grab a hot cup, bowl or plate. Hood over head, hands in your pockets. Initial on the locket or ring. Anything that's empowering, witness the blessings showering upon you and your loved ones. A feeling as if you could launch a hundred rocket all at once.

Which by the way, might as well crash, be prepared for it too. You are capable of building everything from scratch. You do it all the time, without sometimes realizing that.

Basically keep it warm, sing a happy song, or just listen. You will see shattered dreams getting intact and aligned together again slowly.

There is no secret code on the road to success. Stay passionately disciplined at your flex. You'll prove them wrong later, while you have the right mind-set and take the right steps now.

Today, take a vow to rise and shine after every trip, slip, sleep or even fall. You always come back stronger, afterall. ☺

- AZR

Dear Influencer

You make us smile and relate to the things we quiz ourselves with. You become influential when you have the guts to speak out on the lenses. Everybody turns out to be an influencer at some point. It takes time to realize this.

You get followed and been made role-models. With that follows a bunch of responsibilities, honours and powers. Make sure to not mis-use it. If you do, apologize and accept it.

Your face, contents and personality are liked, followed, shared and subscribed every now and then, with contributions you make to the real lives or media. Get watched and let people join your tribe, some call it ridiculous and hysteria when it's just your charisma.

It drives zillions at times. Criticisms are going to be pointed out anyway. You do your best everyday.

You are in a nuptial with the work. Few see you over-work and shrunk in those dark moments.

It's the story of every person. But it's more about who's comfortable sharing the details of life.

Never lose track of your sleep. To carve your best work of art, job or business, don't you starve and work like a creep.

Everything is worth it, if it satisfies your soul and makes you happy. Take those necessary breaks in between and resume with fresh energy.

''You are your own boss'', it's a cool phrase to hear and say but hard to act like you are.

Pressure monitors consistency and makes it a routine. We all have a unique way of shining.

Bother much about what is your original thinking.

Fascinated by the way you glitter. Illusion of effortless recognition loiters in some corners of the internet but always remember, those who judge, never got a chance to see your behind the scenes so just let it be and live peacefully and do your thing.

- AZR

Buddy Note, You're Top-Notch!

Note this buddy, you're my ally for life. Not allowed to lie to me or hide when you're in pain. I'll be that shelter in the rain.

You see how our stars align, you know we don't need to shine together all the time. You got nothing to prove. We improve either way.

You read my face, I squeeze a bit. A good amout of warmth I feel. Your care is rare. You point out my flaws to correct me, that's your coolest dare.

When you understand the silence, and give advice that's honest. It's a license only you have received.

We are music to each other's souls. Dancing to similar tunes. We boost one another's mood, spirit and ever-ready to play our roles.

You're my pal, I definitely crawl to you somehow in my sad and baffled hours. You shower me with your wisdom and love, that's visible even without a touch.

Just to sit with you or sip something with you in our cups filled to the brim. As we spill and overflow our thoughts, ideas and feelings.

Buddy just note, that you're top-notch. We might not get involved every now and then but you're always on my watch.

- AZR

Filter-Out

There is light in our pockets, bunch of rockets about to launch. But when it comes to our benefits or we wish to drag someone down, we simply filter out.

Practising consciousness now, we continue to take a bow. We know the limits, but we wish to go over them and simply want to shout.

We get tired of explaining. We notice the designs falling. We shut up or we snap. When it happened to us, we simply filtered out.

When beliefs stop working for one's advantage, we usually figure out the next step. We step up and articulate. What to say and not. To defend or to just walk out.

One beaten by logic, the other by stupidity. Yet without a doubt, we let our opinions formed and out.

Without understanding the depth by empathy, we let our own ideologies cancel out.

We protest for interpose. But we act opposite. We deal with things accordingly and let our feelings filter out. That's our trick, a defense mechanism, we've learned the art to simply filter-out.

- AZR

Lickspittle

Accuse me of being a lickspittle

Make it look like it's wrong to hold the kettle or the door for others or elders that are strangers.

What's the choice, if the good one has the authority? I don't have a voice for everything. I can't unneccessarily dislike people and question their integrity.

It made me want to change my city, but I didn't. I fought, didn't let their idea rot my mind completely. Perhaps a little, but didn't let that mind-set in.

I can't be you, you can't be me. Is it individuality or a tragedy? I don't go around swearing upon my boss for just being it.

I should look inside, for my own faults. If I can be kind to a mean person, I'm obliged to be great to a good one.

You just got to think. Some are raised with manners. It's how parents are treated at home but we end up acting human.

Perfection is a myth, it is an illusion. Tell me I'm old school. I might just wonder if you've been to a damn school.

Maybe you over-looked the assignments and had super fun instead. Judge me and I will tell your history. Love me and I'll turn out to be the greatest mystery.

- AZR

Careful Cross-Culture

The pictures we had seen in books and inside our dreams and then one day on the internet that probably made us scream from within. "I wanna be there someday. It's my dream!"

When the moment comes to manifest the goals that had been set for years. The naïve side of us is what awaits on the other side, I guess.

Walking in a foreign land was about dealing with its people in the end. Some mean and some really kind.

To mix and become like them without losing oneself and one's identity in the process. It is a challenge, most people struggle with and eventually give up or give in.

Trying to understand, adapt, impress, practise things a bit not alike.

Sadly, multi-coloured stones are admired. The case is not always same with people.

Some generous and others hesitant. Some just won't let us shine through.

Some make us feel we're different on our face, some in disguise and secret.

Cross-culture is beautiful

But one needs to with it, be careful too. 'Cause no one openly shares the bad things they go through.

- AZR

Are We?

Are we too attached to the device in our hands? Has it detached us from making real connections and executable plans? Are we addicted on this unknown land?

Are we unnecessarily taking a step back from going out, from feeling the morning sun on our skin and healing from every other little thing that nature has to provide within.

Are we treating a gizmo like oxygen or a magical wand or ring? Is it a curse instead and poisonous in the long-run thing? All our people from different walks of life gathered through one medium but mostly unaware of each other's true emotions.

Are we too comfortable with this idea and end up being lonely and less productive than we could be? Than we should be?

Are we going to change this soon or end up in the colossal doom. Are we going to take steps to fight this addiction by picking up a book, be it fiction or a non-fiction or cook a meal for our beloved.

Too much of anything is bad even it is known to be good. Why don't we just take a stroll inside the well known woods.

Let's make sure to leave our gadget in a place from time to time. Breathe free and take a moment away from this sort of crime inorder to compose a rhyme or by doing some activity that we really like.-

- AZR

Leave Strong

Often people say, stay strong and in that there is nothing wrong. But I wonder if things would be better if our people made us strong before they were gone?

Nothing in life is permanent but life in itself is temporary. We have a desire to make a difference in the world but what about our own beloved boundaries?

Every sigh has a meaning. Either about hopelessness or finishing a work. What am I living for?

It's not a question but the final curse.

There is a fine line between negativity and reality, just like positivity and over-confidence. One could save us, the other could drown us.

Are we trying to solve a problem by adding a new one? Is it worth it to stay strong all the time or leave strong, or just stay by the side, at the right moment and time?

- AZR

A Year Ago...

A year ago, you felt nowhere close to what you have achieved and where have you reached now. You never imagined all the day dreams could come true.

And well it did, most unexpectedly. So it feels unreal at times, that you made it real this time. Now be certain of what you're capable of and let your potential flow.

The glow Is mystical on your face. Your mystery is unfolding now. Every new year you get a dose of blessings in the form of love, belief and hope to make you stronger, wiser plus dope.

As you held on-to the rough rope, you opened yourself new doors and the tables and chairs are piled up with memories that are rare.

A year has passed and all things astonishingly are differing now. It's clearer view and brighter days. Time to sow a new seed. A chance to show more grit.

The cycle repeats and low moments are inevitable but you're consistently growing and a brand new year is just around the corner.

- AZR

Loss

Life is uncertain and loss is certain. Make sure to toss it out soon, the empty feeling of becoming sentimental. Restart with the same spirit and carry on 'cause that's what our loved ones really want.

With that loss comes a gloss of faith plus patience. May the good fellows and friends cross our path in all seasons. Not particularly for a specific reason but to share kindness and love for brief sessions.

At dawn, some magic exists for sure. A new beginning without them on a physical note but remember that they live in our blood clots and there is a part of them in us and interesting stories still left to uncover.

With that grief, comes moments of groaning. We moan bit too much. The mind is doomed with darkness but it's better to keep a clear head, look forward & trust in God's plan as there is hope for relief at that very moment.

The fear of losing a dear one, a really near one is not easy but do not fear life whilst that and remind yourself of what they really want.

- AZR

The Captain Age

That age has finally arrived of converting theory into practice, where certain goals just can't be missed and mistakes to admit. Where you don't get to choose the cruise and handed over the wheel to deal with, along lifeboats and jackets.

Now life is less about the captions on our handles, and more about becoming the captain of our ships, that is, relationships to handle with care. We try our best indeed, but it could often sink in the blink of an eye and take a couple years to sink-in, the storm and questions like, why me? And answers like, I'll have to carry on. The reality struck that some desires only die and shrink in the storm without being warm.

The age when one stops growing up and starts growing older. Maybe now is the perfect time to offer and lend a shoulder. And a legit reason to hold her, that little girl in pink who is far away from the stink of the world. Who can't yet differentiate between types of winks, the king and leaders. Their hardships and sins.

The globe is fully designed. It weighs me down, and forces me to lay there unwillingly too, sometimes in pain, where there is nothing to gain as only confusion and meaninglessness remains.

And oh, I think to myself, when did that happen? The rain that I loved the most, stopped making sense. Is growing up a curse to begin with in the first place? Not enjoying it anymore, just getting wet.

The pink sky turning eventually grey. When the dark night surpasses the vibrant day ending up merging together. Maybe that's the law of nature.

What am I going to do, when the sun shines again the next day? I ask myself repetitively. I might take a U-Turn and think like a child again and ignore the sense of life again. Because even when stories and movies must do that, real life doesn't always make sense. The dark is dense and tensed, but the morning will be clear and full of sweet scents. Along with some partnerships. Another chance might be given to turn things around with near and dear ones.

The wisdom to never make a final decision on temporary feelings and events might help.

So I'm just going to pretend like the captain of my ship, my life, and keep it afloat and avoid from drowning.

- AZR

Unspoken Words Again

Unspoken words again came to life in writing. A blank page is filled with unexpressed emotions and ideas again. Assisting in clarity of thoughts and helping to tie sanity knots that are vibrant.

Some ideals that seemed to be lost which nearly made to pay the cost. Why have I been ignoring the space that gives me peace & brings me back to a safer environment?

Like a clot that was frozen still, I let it all release and radiate through my bones & skin. I've always known the drill. Always heard that the skills pay the bills.

Always been someone who minds the tones more than the words or the moans.

Hands stained with ink again, leaves my fingertips pink again. Makes me think after I let those sweet & sad feelings sink again.

Just content that I'm back to what made me feel better and more alive. May it turn amongst the best choice. Doesn't matter if sometimes leaves my eyes moist. There's a kind of pleasure in the pain. There's a treasure beneath, I have gained.

Unspoken words will never feel the same. But it can help me to devour and stay sane without my energy being drained by the world again and again.

- AZR

Not ''Just'' Humble

Surely stay humble, but not to the extent that you stumble & no one comes to rescue until you eventually crumble and fade away. Mentally, they shall dump you like litter, the real flex might be perhaps that, it does not leave your existence any bitter.

Pick that dumble up if you could, show them their place if you should. Say things that would save some that come after you, even if it starts with a mumble & makes you fumble & leaves your life jumbled up in the moments of truth and forces you into a deep slumber and then a list of comments thrown at you after a huge bummer.

One day you shall be wide awake after the come-back you make for God's sake. Pick yourself up after that slump. You won't regret a bit.

Let go of that lump in your throat. You will get another chance to wear those coats & shirts with collars. Sit once again among the company of scholars or old wise men & women, who share knowledge & don't expect much in return. Who help you grow while you don't even know.

Be patient & humble with them if that's a trait that you really possess.

The world eats up the humble.

Stay not just humble and do not let anyone cross the boundary.

Make it pristine, humble not weak, kind not stupid, good not timid. Caring not someone who doesn't recognize when you're taking them for granted.

Never enough to just stay humble in a world which is designed to constantly crumble whatever goodness remains. Protect those emotions or resurrect if it's dead. Being just humble all the time, just isn't safe.

- AZR

Teacher's Sign

A special sign that plays major roles in the lives of young & immature souls within a delicate phase of that innocent face, with red ink, the numbers, stars and moon can boost so much of confidence so soon & get a child out of doom. Like a super-power thing, they hold in their pen & the chalks like the words they utter and sing while they walk in the corridors & shrink.

Conduct given ''good'' even if it wasn't. Those signs of a kind & caring heart we sense in subjects like social science and others, that go beyond the classroom lessons while they share some vital & heart-warming experience.

Instructions leading to formation & construction of our thoughts and beliefs. A teacher is the only one who comes to our relief with a cheerful face and a passionate energy. Always eager

& happy to help in all it's real sense.

The handwritten & printed notes, the steps & formulas, the maps, graphs, journals. Imprinted are their quotes & dialogues of clarifying every single doubt & making sure no one's left behind.

Our vote goes out for a teacher, who has worked relentlessly for the welfare of students and improved several generations. A greatly satisfying job for the lifetime after completing all the academic tasks and missions.

Let's not be the ones who ungratefully blame the education system. And make those sacrifices, dedication and exposure given to us count. Who always made sure we were safe and sound when our families weren't around.

Teachings have obviously shaped us and I could go on and on.

To end this, it all started with a Teacher's Sign, which I always wanted to be mine because it shines through million lives.

The difference they make is visible and deep. Departed from amazingly talented teachers year after year. Still sometimes when I get down, while handling life, a Teacher's Sign is all that I seek to motivate me and bring me back to my peak.

- AZR

Are The Rich Always Privileged?

The pressure might be real on the rich to achieve higher than their natural pitch. Who struggle to stitch on time because ease was passed onto them as a gift. To stay away from the deadly ditch leads to a huge payment of price, sometimes.

No one talks about this 2nd generation sacrifice. Assuming effortlessly getting that meat on their rice over a golden plate & a silver spoon with perfect salt and spice. What's the point of being so nice to their silent cries & resistance. Is it wise to wait until their tear finally dries and fades away?

The ones who are needed to be trained, untamed, unlearn and are unskilled on a certain level. As if growing cash on tree was a true concept leads to a mind that is forever free or empty concept.

As if to give was a duty & there couldn't be any beauty in that or what mattered was only the surface. The ones expected to perform better & more than the survival with bare minimum squad.

Is It always fair to say that the rich are privileged? Escaping the do or die but caught up in do or follow thy shoe. With all the availability of luxury and distractions, isn't it challenging to have that kind of attention & hardwork?

Responsibilities laid on them to provide for the welfare of the community & society at large. Can't we genuinely respect the section of the unapplauded benevolence of the rich who often give up what's more comfortable & convenient to them and juggle between the unpredictable struggles too?

When there are so many choices that one could get lost and baffled. Aren't they deserving of stories to be heard and the ones battled.Too much sophistication & protection leading to suffocation of individuality. Maybe they are the ones who might need our help too & also underprivileged on a scale that is unimaginably true.

- AZR

Dutifully Beautiful

Sometimes I don't know what to say to the beauty standards set for women that draws them closer to a cage. It's mind boggling to see the imports of cosmetics, forces me to think about common ethics.

It's funny & a very serious problem, since ads & their tag lines made us believe that. That

God made us imperfectly on outward. ''Now let's make some experiments with chemicals on your skin''.

Education also goes astray on this topic for some exterior reasons, I believe. The companies are trying to sell their products well, in the market to get their share of profit.

The more natural you are, the prettier the looks. Cause honestly we are not trying to look like a vampire or a witch illustrated in the books. The dark lipstick or the powder in your skin. Get it for you, if you want to, for yourself. But never inorder to fit into the cruel standard the society or your community has set.

It's sad to see this sort of ignorance. I pray & hope it gets better without a sign of warning. Is It really a duty of a woman or young female adult to look ''beautiful'' like that. When it all really does look like is plastic. I'm not even being sarcastic. I mean this from the bottom of my heart.

Save modelling men & women from this kind of curse, which will eventually drain out whatever is left in their purse. Be dutiful in acts of kindness, worship, care & completion of the tasks. Dare to be your truly self without those visible masks. Believe, you are beautiful the way you are.

- AZR

59

Deeper Oceans

A blessing or a curse? To think and feel deeply to the verge of a breaking point. Busy in joining the dots that leaves a big vacant hole behind.

When saying ''yes'' only seems like the right option. A series of dilemma leading to filtered noble adoptions. They're human afterall. Only able to take that call. Confined within four walls might be their one-sided thoughts.

Unaware of their past, might be a valid reason for that kind of behaviour. Kind to the unkind. Later just unwind & become one's own saviour.

If taking an advantage is the law & pattern. ''we'' and 'they'' would've been a constant message & dialogue passing down like a generational curse or a blessing that says, for ''all of us''.

Does it make sense & instill values over a period of time? Or it goes to waste like every single cry?

A list of questions dwelling in the mind. Doing the wrong, while understanding the clarity of right.

There is a belief that there is an ocean of deep thinkers. That there is always a solution if you sincerely sought in every direction. Not be left done with the outdated ideas & believe in individuality and it's unique fun.

Then happiness wouldn't appear so numb on them. Perhaps, they would dream too. Even after a harsh phase, they might not have a hard heart & a dark soul.

Often asked in the concept of emotions. How deep is your love for this & that or someone?

Hope that no one is delusional when answering that kind of question.

- AZR

61

Pace Out

Learn things at your pace, nothing should be defined by age. Anything conducted regularly shall catch speed. It's just a matter of hardcore practise. That can help match you up with anyone and anything.

Some learn fast, some take time. Some change their minds, depending upon the situations in life. Who am I to judge you? Even if I do, it shouldn't matter to you. Keep your head high.

Try not to lie, to yourself atleast. You will figure out, without a doubt.

There are plenty of ways to get there. Stuck phases too have hopes of ray that you might want to share as well. Keep courage to keep thoughts clear and eyes wide. After that drawback, perhaps it's your time to shine. Never give up on your stride. Never let go of that spark. It's going to definitely assist you in the dark.

Surrounded by people who love you, you'd stretch yourself for them real soon. From kitchen to corporate, every task you can manage, ace and fully operate. Forget for a while at what rate and on which date. By encouragement & care, everyone can drastically change for good.

Become better and finally their best.

Someone has always been taking care of the rest. Don't worry about your pace or theirs.

Focus on yourself first and lectures last.

Action is the key. Thinking too much can be paralytic. Pace could be slow, but shall not stop your flow to grow, if you keep moving ahead. Live in peace and keep that pace out for once and every once in a while. Either you walk or drive, you are always capable of reaching every mile.

- AZR

63

Jewel Hearts

Peculiar feature of a jewel heart is that it secretly rules a million hearts, alike and different. Seems like a mystical craft to ones who acknowledge. Attract and distract some too. Grateful to have them around and wishes to surround themselves, forever true. Like an ordinary chain turning into a fine gold thread and wishes goodness so that it bred.

Then comes the second and the most common category. That has their face red at the sight of well behaved. Since, the other thing about a jewel heart is it soon intimidates a cruel heart since it slows down its pace of negativity.

The ones who work according to mood and act good as per their convenience of you and judge on the basis of your face value. The ones who hallucinate without being sick as they kick and push aside the goodness sent to their path as they sneak out of the conversation with cunning statements and benefit of doubts.

Little do they know, that the world is wide and life might be long, that not all remain under the hide. At least not from the glittery omnipresent eyes. Someone's lies are someone's cries.

Must've been that wise and a bit nice. Preferring authenticity over witty and dirty play.

Anyways, everyone makes mistakes and jewel hearts aren't excluded from it. As they deal with the rude with modesty, somehow believe to help them heal responsibly. Always on feet for the ones who ride constantly on wheels even if the covering distance was short plus sweet. And skip the meal to instill good and make good look appealing for someone who doesn't care at all.

Those hearts snap for a justified reason. They've been putting a lot of their emotions into prison.

The funny part is, they feel sorry even for those who wronged. Also, after they've been gone.

Regrets stay along for a longer period of time without a valid crime.

That's when you realize that you recently had an encounter with a jewel heart. Which was far from usual and everything set them apart because they had a class which was beyond the understanding of a mediocre mass.

- AZR